Science CE/KS3
Topic Booklet

Working Scientifically

Improvements:

Beakers have lips so they are not sealed.

An improvement would be to use jars.

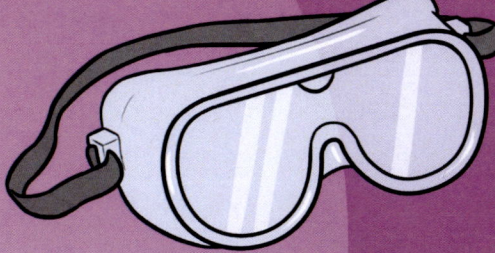

- Read, engage and learn!
- Full colour, illustrated Topic Booklet.
- Glossary of key words, Active Learning Game & Flashcards.
- Ideal for ISEB 13+ Common Entrance and KS3 pupils.

This Oaka™ Books Topic Booklet goes hand in hand with the Active Learning Pack on this topic. The pack includes a Write Your Own Notes Booklet, an Active Learning Game and Question & Answer flashcards.

Fresh Focus on Learning

Working Scientifically Glossary

 **Accurate**: correct information.

Compare: to show how things are similar or different.

Conclusion: a few sentences to show how your results agree or disagree with your hypothesis.

 **Control variables**: things or amounts that you will keep the same.

Dependent (output) variable: the bit you measure and is affected during an experiment.

 **Equipment**: the necessary items for a particular purpose.

Evaluation: comparing one set of results against another. Thinking about what worked best and why.

 **Experiment**: a test under controlled conditions to test a hypothesis.

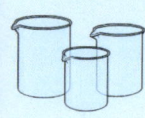 **Fair Test**: changing only one thing at a time during an experiment.

 **Hypothesis**: an idea or explanation to be tested in an experiment.

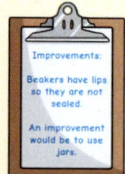 **Improvement**: an action that makes something better.

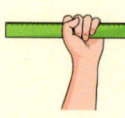 **Independent variable**: a variable that is changed in an experiment.

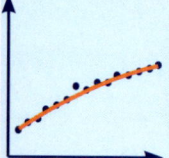 **Line of Best Fit**: a line drawn through as many points as possible on a graph.

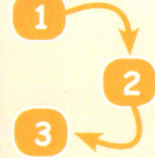 **Measurements**: the size, length or amount of something.

Method: a way of doing something in an ordered sequence of fixed steps.

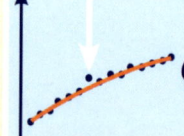 **Outliers**: an odd result.

 **Reliability**: where an experiment shows similar results when repeated.

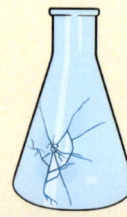 **Risk Assessment**: evaluating the potential risks in an experiment.

Conducting An Experiment

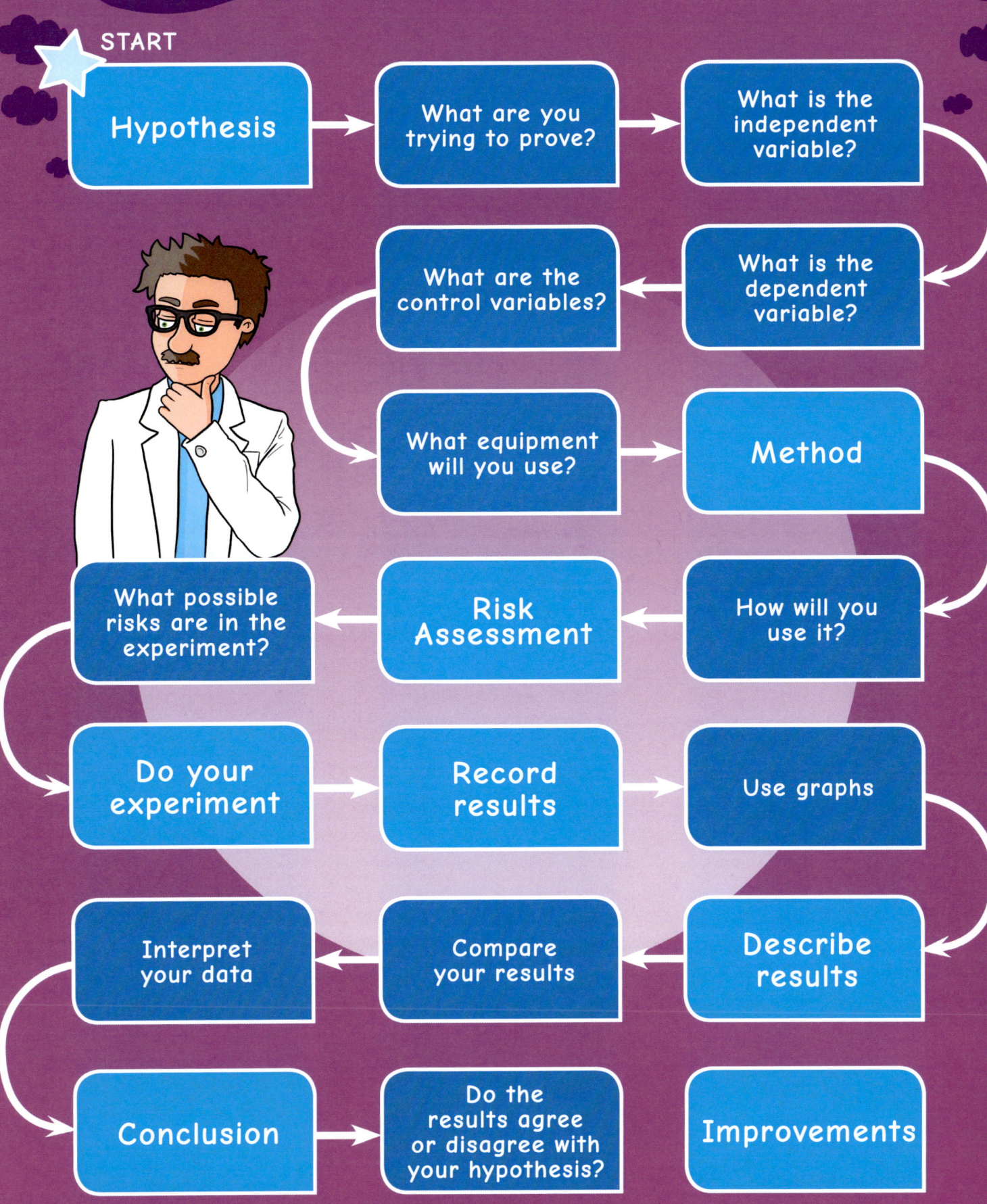

Working Scientifically

1   Why Does That Happen?

- Scientists try to work out **why** things happen.

Why can one person jump higher than another?

Why can one car go faster than another?

Why does one cow produce more milk than another?

2   Guessing

- We can **guess** a reason.
- But it may or may not be true.
- That's because it has not been proven.

I guess that....

3   Hypothesis (hipe-oth-ess-sis)

- This means that the guess is just a possible reason.
- Scientists call it a **hypothesis**.

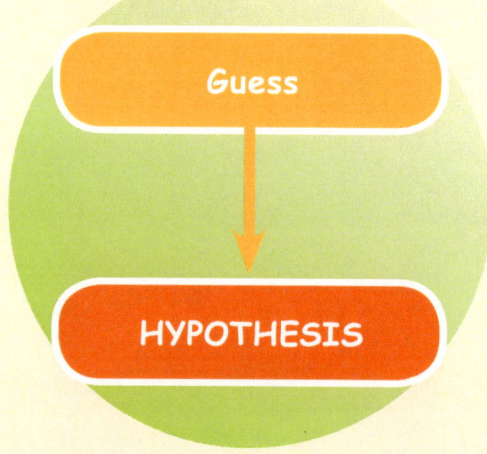

Guess

HYPOTHESIS

Working Scientifically

4   Is The Hypothesis True?

- So, how do we work out if a **hypothesis** is **true or not**?
- We **conduct** (do) an **experiment**.

Let's conduct an experiment!

5   What Is An Experiment?

- It is the **collection** of **data** (information).
- This will tell us if the hypothesis is true or not.

6   The Aim

- Before you start an experiment, you need to have an **aim** (the **hypothesis**).
- What are you trying to **prove**?

7   My experiment is...

- Make your aim about one thing.
- Do say: 'My experiment is to investigate the effect of sunlight on the growth of a plant.'

Variables

8 Don't Make It General

- **Do not** say 'I'm going to look at how plants grow.'
- This is too **general**.
- If you change more than one thing, it will not be a fair test.

Make sure to be specific!

9 Making Experiments Count

Experiments need to be:

Fair

Accurate

Able to be repeated

10 What is a Variable?

- Anything in an experiment that we can **measure** is called a **variable**.

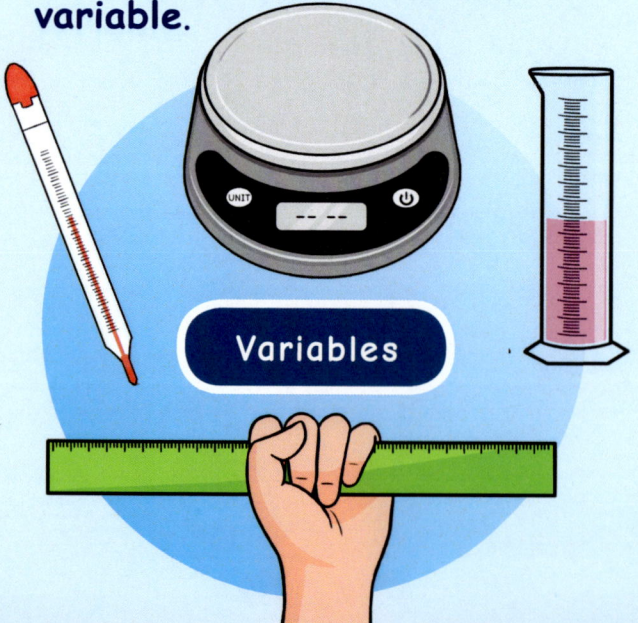

Variables

11 Things That Change

- There are **independent** (also known as input) **variables**.
- These are things than we can change.

What can I change in my experiment?

Variables

12 Things That Are Affected

- There are **dependent** (or output) **variables**.
- These are **changed** by the **independent** variable.

The more sunlight (the input variable) there is...

...the bigger the plant grows (output variable)

13 Choosing One Thing

- If you were investigating the effect of light on plant growth, the **independent variable** could be:

"The number of <u>hours of light</u> the plant is given each day."

14 Things That Stay The Same (Control Variables)

- There are things that are **not changed**.
- These are the **control variables**.
- Things that would **stay** the **same** (**control variables**) would be:

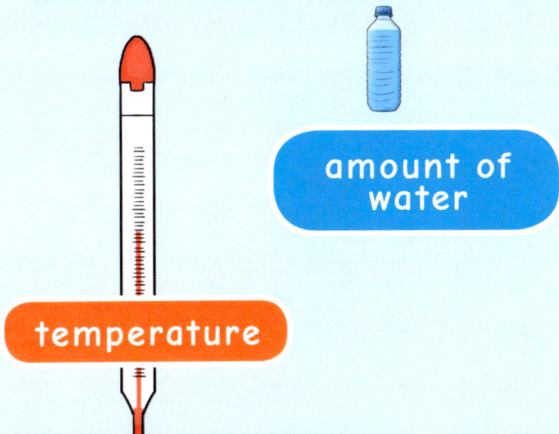

temperature

amount of water

pro-grow SOIL

amount of soil used

type of soil used

type of plant used

Variables

15 The Dependent Variable

- The **dependent variable** (or output variable) will be the **growth** of the **plant**.

- So growth will be affected (changed) by the **amount of light** it is **given**.

dependent variable = growth of the plant

16 A Fair Test

To make your **experiment** a **fair test** you need to:

only change one variable at a time!

17 A Reliable Result = Average Readings

- **Repeat** your experiment.

- Take an **average reading**. Add up your results and divide then by the number of times you have done the test:

5cm   6cm   7cm

- If your plant grew 5cm on the first test, 7cm on the second and 6cm on the third.

- Add 5cm + 6cm + 7cm = 18cm

- 18cm divided by 3 = 6cm

6cm is the average growth!

Taking Measurements

18 Equipment

- Use the right equipment to measure variables.
- Accurate measurements are important.
- Measure on flat surfaces.

WRONG!

CORRECT!

19 Ruler

- Use rulers for measuring length.
- Measure from 0 mm.

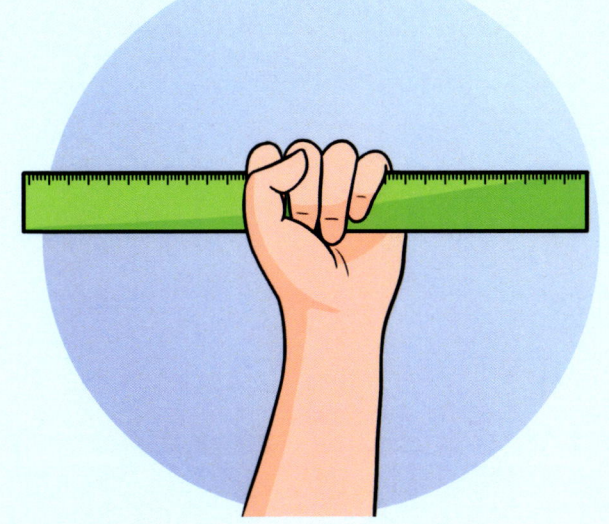

20 Glass or Plastic?

- Use glass beakers for hot liquids.
- Plastic beakers can melt or change shape.

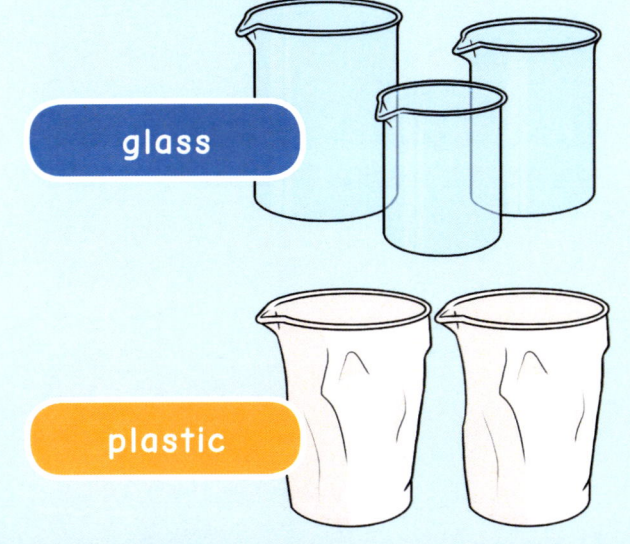

glass

plastic

21 Measuring Liquids

- Use measuring cylinders for measuring liquids.
- Measure the flat part of the liquid.

Measuring Liquids

22   Measuring Liquids

- If you measure liquid, remember:

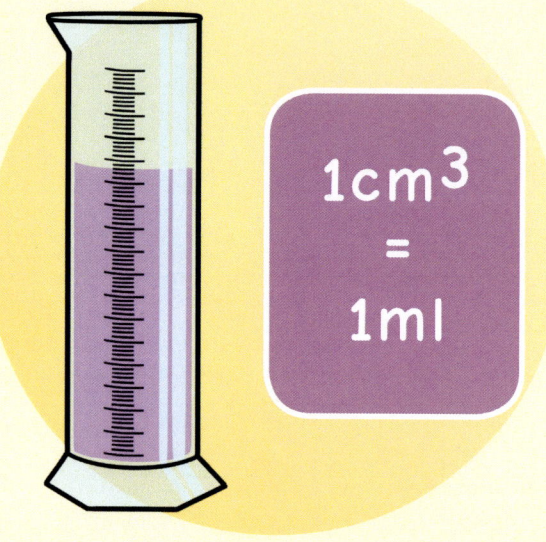

$$1cm^3 = 1ml$$

23   Weighing Solids

- If you weigh a solid in a dish, you need to:
- Weigh the dish (A).

A

24   Weighing Solids

- Weigh the dish with the solid (B).

B

25   Weighing Solids

- Take away A from B.

$$B - A = Xg$$

- X is the mass of the solid.

Risk Assessment

26   What Are The Risks?

Think about all the **possible risks**:

- Burns from a bunsen burner.

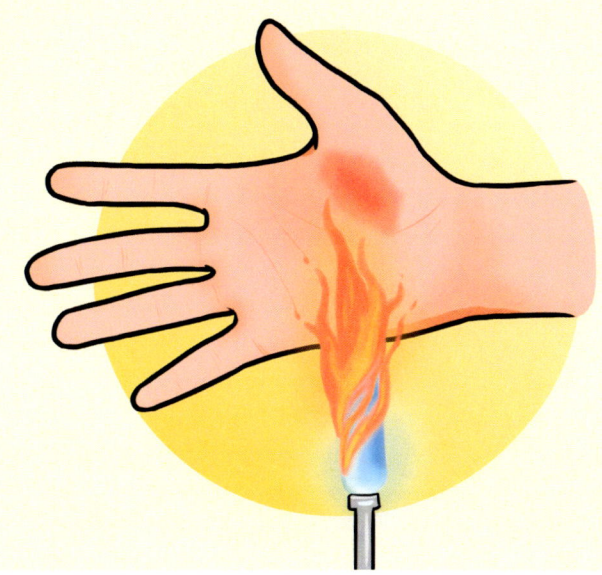

27   Long Hair

- Burning long hair.

28   Spilt Chemicals

- Getting **chemicals** in your eye.

29   Glass Breaking

- Danger of a test tube or beaker **breaking**.

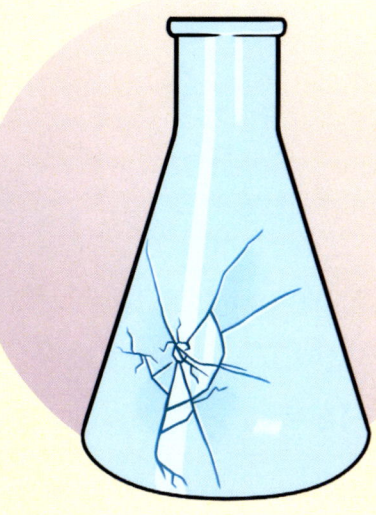

Reducing The Risks

30 Safety Clothing

- Wear an **apron**.
- Take care with naked flames.

31 Working Safely

- Tie back long hair.
- No dangling shirt sleeves.

32 Safety Goggles

- Wear **safety goggles**.
- Keep lids on chemical bottles.

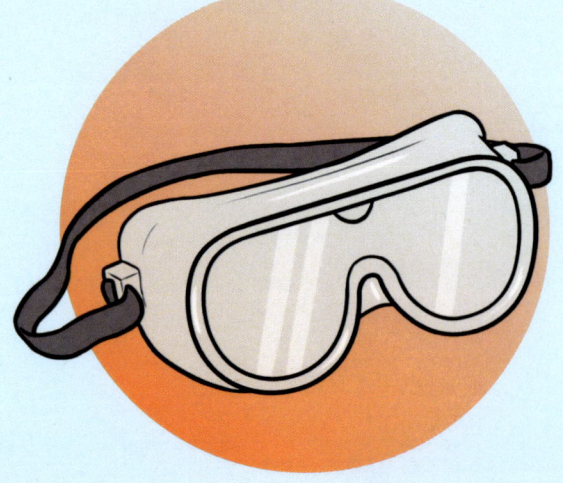

33 Using Equipment

- Don't make clamps too tight.
- Put beakers on flat surfaces.

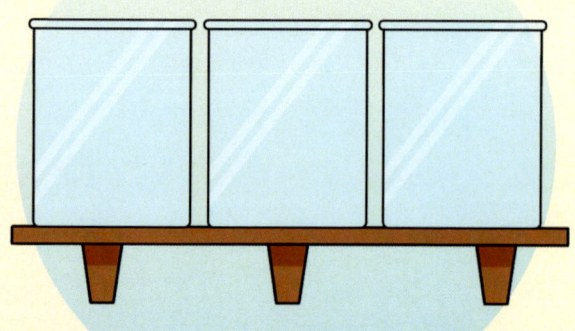

Conducting An Experiment

34   An Investigation

- Let's carry out an experiment.
- The process will be the same for any experiment you do.

Time to experiment!

35   Hypothesis

- First write your **hypothesis**.
- This could be '**I think that the amount of oxygen will affect how long a candle burns**'.

36   Independent Variable

- Now we need to see if it is true!
- Identify the **independent variable** (the bit you will **change**).
- This could be the size of the beaker you put your candles in.

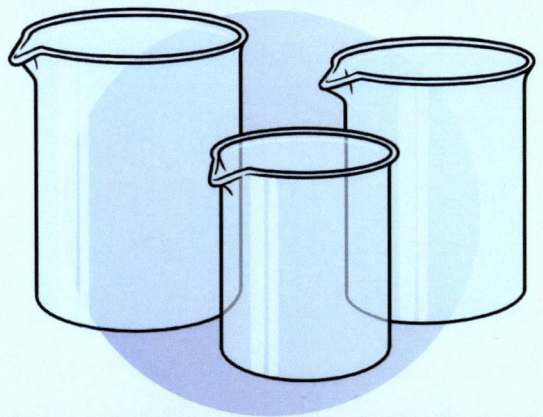

37   Dependent Variable

- Identify the **dependent variable** (the thing that will be changed by the independent variable).
- This is the time it takes for the candle to go out.

Conducting An Experiment

38 — What is the control variable?

- This is using the same type and size of candle for each test.

39 — Write a Method

What equipment will you use?

- different sized beakers.
- tea lights.
- stopwatch.
- heat proof mat.

40 — How will you use it?

- Place a tea light on a heat proof mat.

- Light it and place a beaker over it.

41 — Repeat the Experiment

- Time how long it takes for the candle to go out.

- Repeat for each of the beakers.

- Then repeat your experiment.

- Work out an average of the results.

Conducting An Experiment

 **42**   **Making it a fair test**

- **Remember**: make sure you **only** change **one variable** at a time during the experiment.

- In this experiment, it will be the beakers.

43   **The Results**

- Plan your table of results.

- What will you measure?

beaker size   time taken

 **44**   **Identify the Risks**

Make a table for your risk assessment.

What is the risk?	The dangers	Reducing the risk

45   **Do the Experiment**

- Now you can do the experiment and put your results in the table.

Beaker size	Time taken

Displaying The Results

46   Drawing a Graph

• Use a sharp pencil and a ruler.

Remember:
x axis - independent variable.
y axis - dependent variable.

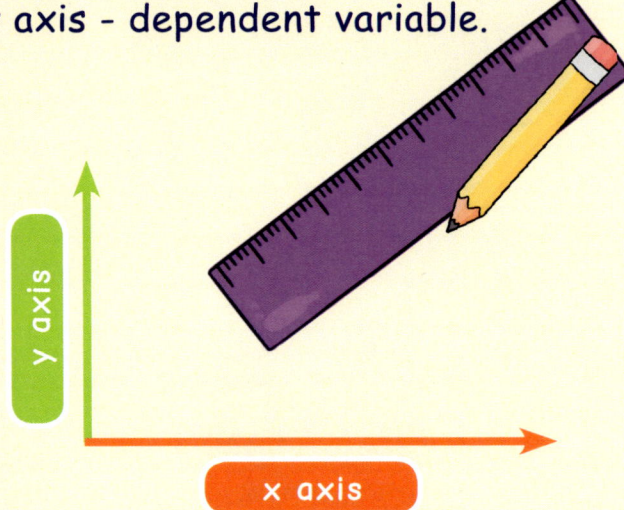

47   Which Graph?

• For this experiment we have numbers for both variables.

• So, a **line graph** is best.

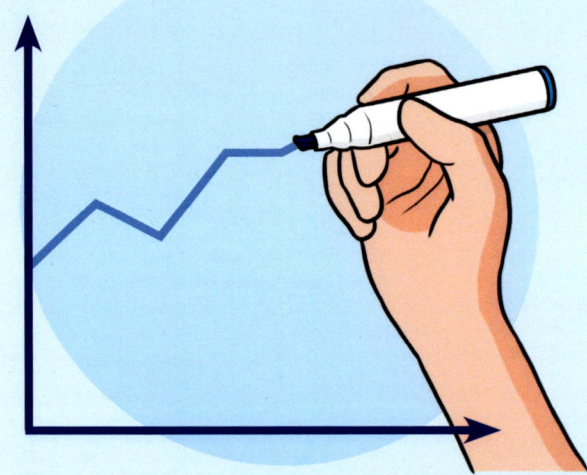

48   Bar Chart

• Remember: if you had only **one variable** that was numbers then a **bar chart** would be best.

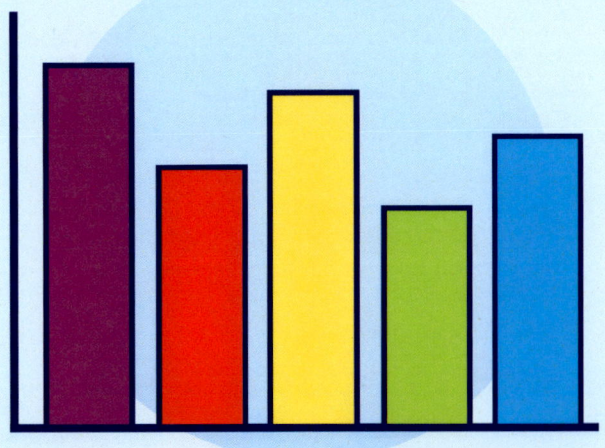

49   Line of Best Fit (not required for CE)

• On your line graph draw the **line of best fit.**

• Go through as many points as possible.

• The line can be straight **or** curved.

line of best fit

This booklet is not to be photocopied. Thank you.

What Do Your Results Show?

50 Odd Results (not required for CE)

- The line of best fit will show any **odd results**.

- These are called **outliers**.

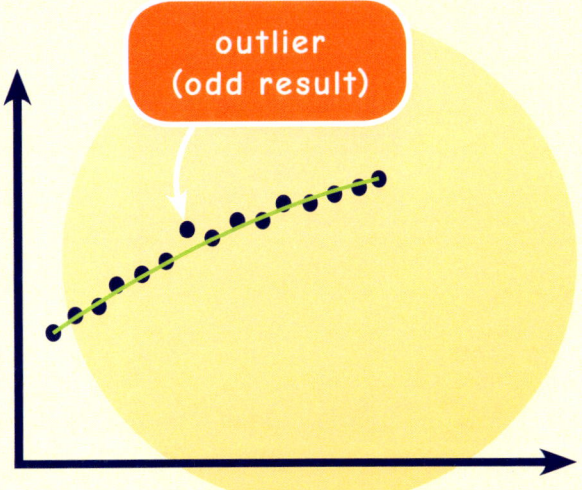

51 Describe The Results

- Write a sentence to explain the results.

- My results show that the flame lasts longest in the largest beaker.

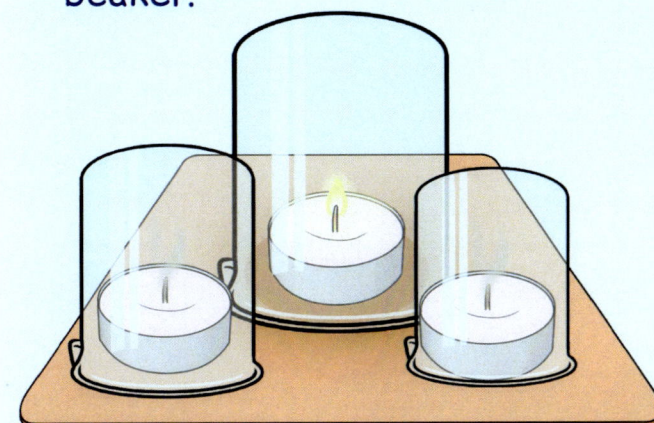

52 Compare The Results

- How long did the flame last in each of the beakers? Give details.

> In the 500ml beaker, the flame lasted x seconds.
>
> In the 300ml beaker, the flame lasted y seconds.
>
> Whereas in the 150ml beaker, it only lasted z seconds.

53 Now explain what you saw (Conclusion)

- Why do you think this happened?

> The flame lasted longest in the biggest beaker because there was more oxygen.

- This is OK and will get you some marks BUT....

Conclusion and Improvement

54 — Go For More Marks!

- A better conclusion might be:

The 500ml beaker had the largest volume of oxygen.

This meant that the candle could burn for longer as oxygen is needed for combustion.

As the candle burned, CO_2 was produced and O_2 was used up.

This took longer in the biggest beaker because there was more oxygen to start with.

55 — How could you improve the experiment?

Think about how you could make your experiment better and why!

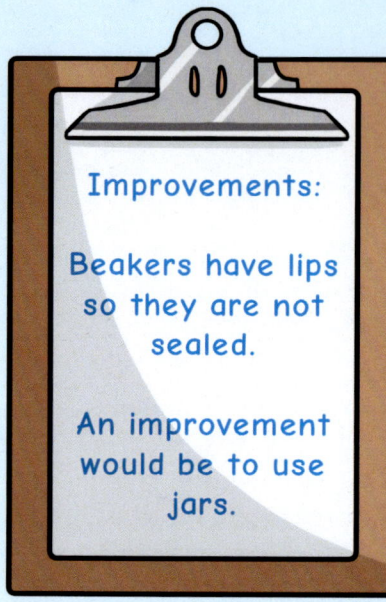

Improvements:

Beakers have lips so they are not sealed.

An improvement would be to use jars.

56 — How did you make it a reliable test?

- The experiment was done 3 times for each of the independent variables (the size of the beaker).

- This made the results more reliable.

Repeated 3 times

57 — How did tou make it a fair test?

- Just one variable was changed.

Conducting An Experiment

Aim (What are you trying to prove?):

Independent Variables (What will you change?):

Dependent Variables (What is going to change?):

Control Variables (What will you keep the same?):

Equipment (What will you use?):

Method (How will you do the experiment?):

Conclusion (What happened?):

Evaluation (How did the results compare with the different independent variables?):

Improvement (What could you do to make the experiment more reliable?):

About Oaka Books

Children learn best when they are engaged...

Our aim is to help children enjoy learning by making it fun! That way they will succeed.

This Topic Pack is based on the ISEB 13+ Common Entrance and National Curriculum guidelines for KS3.

The design and layout of our books follow guidelines from the British Dyslexia Association.

Three Easy Steps

Read: the easy to follow bullet point Topic Booklet.

Engage: Play the Active Learning Game.

Learn: When you understand the topic, test yourself using the Write Your Own Notes Book. You can use the Topic Booklet to help if you get stuck.

One (short) Topic at a time:

For some students, a big book is a big turn off. That's why we focus on one topic at a time. Short and to the point.

Reading Age

This booklet is suitable for children with a reading age of 10 years.

Topic Packs for KS1, KS2 & KS3 Include:

History
Geography
Chemistry
Biology
Physics
Maths
French

Please visit www.oakabooks.co.uk for more information about forthcoming titles

© Copyright 2018 Oaka™ Books. All rights reserved.
Contributor: Stuart Lawes, BSc, PGCE.
Illustrations by Adora Holcroft.

First paperback edition printed 2015 in the United Kingdom.
A catalogue record for this book is available from the British Library.

ISBN 978-1-911189-14-5
No part of this book shall be reproduced or transmitted in any form or by any means, electronic or mechanical, including photocopying, recording or by any information retrieval system without written permission of the copyright owner or a licence permitting restricted copying issued by the Copyright Licensing Agency Ltd, Saffron House, 6-10 Kirby Street, London EC1N 8TS Tel: 020 7400 3100   Fax: 020 7400 3101   Email: cla@cla.co.uk   Web: www.cla.co.uk

Designed, set and published by Oaka™ Books.

To order other titles from Oaka™ Books, please email info@oakabooks.co.uk or visit www.oakabooks.co.uk, or phone: +44 (0) 2392 388519.

Acknowledgements
Our huge thanks go to the many teachers who have been involved in the development of this series of learning guides. Special thanks to Joy Gardiner, for producing hundreds of illustrations, to Kate Doehren, for her enthusiasm and invaluable assistance to my wonderful daughter Sophie, for being the inspiration for the books and, of course, to Charlie, for believing in them.

ISBN 978-1-911189-14-5   Produced in association with Kate Doehren, MA Ed, B.Ed Hons, RSA Dip, Sp LD/Dyslexia
Head of Learning Support, Hurstpierpoint College
© Copyright Oaka™ Books 2018

ISBN 978-1-911189-14-5
9 781911 189145

CE/KS3/KS4
Working Scientifi-
Topic Booklet